Launch to Freedom Workbook

For Aspiring Women Entrepreneurs

ISBN-13: 978-1722988234
ISBN-10: 1722988231

DEDICATION

This book is dedicated to all the hard-working, driven and motivated women willing to take a risk to explore a new world because you know there is something more than the status quo. That notion or gut instinct to launch your idea – listen to it. Building a company can be described with many adjectives but, isn't it better to go through this journey on your own terms than not try at all? Don't get trapped in the gravitational pull and the comfort of the planet where someone else is telling you not only what to do but how to do it. Remember, you always have a choice and it can begin by putting one foot in front of the other each day.

CONTENTS

ABOUT THE INSTRUCTOR
Hope Hartman

When I moved to Fort Collins, Colorado several years ago, I knew it was a place I could call home. Not only is it an approachable city with new businesses popping up each year, but it is also a bubbling entrepreneurial ecosystem. From being raised in Lexington, Kentucky to years spent with theatre groups, I understand firsthand the importance of community. We need circles of support and like-minded people to build our reservoirs, as well as those who think differently to challenge the status quo or to help us articulate WHY we're doing what we do.

I possess a bachelor's degree in psychology and a master's degree in theater, and both of them have informed my work. Overall, I have spent a couple of decades in the business sector working for small, family-owned businesses, large corporations, higher education, non-profits as well as technology startups. My professional experience includes being the vice president of business development at an intellectual property and technology transfer software company in Kirkland, Washington for several years. Most recently I served as the chief operations officer at a digital fundraising software company in Colorado, following my exit from a consulting company I co-founded with my husband, EnConnect Holdings, which was acquired by a Japanese Venture Capital firm. At the writing of this workbook, I held an executive role at a technology startup.

My background also includes teaching experiences such as working with youth English language learners, being a software trainer with Higher Education professionals, and serving as a mentor, coach and facilitator to young women entrepreneurs for one-week intensive accelerator programs.

No matter where my professional career has taken me, I have always known life is all about the journey. My motto is "do it because you can."

INTRODUCTION

"Make the most of yourself by fanning the tiny, inner sparks of possibility into flames of achievement."

- <u>Golda Meir</u>

Have you ever thought about pursuing your own idea and trying to make a living? Do you spend time brainstorming ideas and imagining how great life would be if you could do your own thing? I'm here to tell you it's possible. I've been through this cycle a few times over the years. If you had these thoughts, you have already taken a step forward. Let me explain how it happened to me!

In late 2017, when a neighbor listened to my most current job woes, simply asked, "Have you ever thought about starting your own company?" He and his wife had observed that when people get to a point where they either surpass the leadership at their workplace or have a tendency to want to criticize leadership, and possibly even challenge them in the workplace, it is a strong sign that it is time to try your own thing. I remember when they expressed this because I felt such internal validation for the thoughts I had been having as of late. I heard their message - you have outgrown the situation or it is no longer a good fit. Does this apply to you? If so, then we can relate!

The other instance of this similar conversation was a phone call I was having with my younger brother. I had for the first time in my life spent the morning crying with anger at my current work situation, trying to pull myself together and almost did not pick up the phone because I was in such an infuriated state of mind, however I thought hearing from a family member might perk me up. He of course knew something was wrong right away and when asked I mustered up through choked sobs, "I hate my job, and I'm so sick of this bullshit! I can't do this anymore – I will not do this for another year!"

Being the awesome brother that he is, he immediately started brainstorming ideas while giving me positive compliments about my strengths, encouraging me that I would be able to find another job or that I could lean into my network or get out there and start networking with a purpose. "I know you've done this before with other people, and I'm not saying it wouldn't be a LOT of work but what about starting your own company?" he asked.

Why deny what needs to be done? It was time for me to start taking things into my own hands. This was the moment I started planning the business I launched in 2018. This experience is what inspired me to create this workbook so I could share with you the lessons and experiences I've learned over the years and have seen reinforced recently. I wanted to strike while the iron was hot and the details were fresh and relevant. I want to encourage YOU to start building your own business so you can experience a newfound freedom if that is something you desire and are looking for a simple guide to help you chart your course.

Building a business is not for everyone, however for some of us who have tried various roles and occupations, it is the most natural, sensible and rewarding experience we can possibly imagine.

The premise behind Launch to Freedom is that by *taking a step each day* you can build your business. If time permits you may take 2 or 3 steps in a day; however, some steps will be more involved than others. My goal is to encourage you to devote a minimum of 30 minutes a day for the next few months to prove to yourself that this can be done! Habits form quickly and if you follow this pursuit for a good three months, you will be well on your way to making strides toward creating the life you want.

Taking small steps each day establishes an approach that will allow you to make progress, *which feels good* and is *empowering* since you have made a decision to change your situation as well as being realistic about your time constraints.

Finally, the theme of this workbook is intentional. It is meant to invoke the spirit of a grand adventure. Since incorporating my company as Escape Velocity it was only fitting that my initial endeavor would reference a space journey within the theme. Have fun. Yes, I said have fun in a business startup guide!

How to Use this Workbook

FIND A ONE OR TWO HOUR TIMESLOT WHERE YOU HAVE ACCESS TO A COMPUTER AND THE QUIET OF YOUR OWN THOUGHTS BEFORE YOU BEGIN. READ THE CONTENT AND MOST IMPORTANTLY PURSUE THE ACTIVITIES AND MISSIONS AS INDICATED BY THE ICONS BELOW.

Icon Glossary

Woman on a Mission – a direct challenge for you to take action on what is suggested within the box below the icon.

Freedom Tip – an idea for you to consider; to create new habits, patterns, ways of thinking and approaches so that you can find the balance between life and pursuing your idea.

Activity – sections for you to write down your ideas, thoughts and findings. Consider the ideas presented, complete the activities and apply the learning beyond the workbook.

Objective - the goal behind the presented concept and what you will learn.

All logos are credited to Flaticon.

https://www.flaticon.com/

Shout out to the designers and artists who offer free logo designs. I'll spread the word whenever I can and hopefully have planted a seed for you here!

MODULE 1
IDEATION

"You are the one that possesses the keys to your being. You carry the passport to your own happiness."

- Diane von Furstenberg

This workbook was written to supplement an online course I designed to walk women entrepreneurs through five fundamental modules to begin the journey of building their own businesses. It was designed to expose women to entrepreneurship and business basics to explore and determine if they want to pursue a course of action to become the leaders of their careers. Although it takes time and effort, my philosophy is if you can do one thing every day to move your business idea forward, you are making progress and it will come to fruition. The small step approach, if applied persistently, can yield big results over time.

If the activities in this workbook are pursued in a thoughtful and substantial manner, an aspiring woman entrepreneur could execute them and have the fundamental business pieces in place to launch their entrepreneurship. Let's get started – I'm on your team.

Objectives

As a result of completing the activities in this module you will be able to:

- **Identify business ideas**
- **Appreciate the entrepreneurial challenge**
- **Identify Personal Advisory Team members**
- **Locate relevant Peer Groups**

Activity 1.1

Ideation

The first step to building your own business is working through your ideas and selecting one to focus on and pursue wholeheartedly. In entrepreneurial speak, this process is known as ideation; however, think of it as brainstorming. It may seem like a luxury to you to spend time brainstorming if you're like the majority of other women I know who are trying to balance jobs, homes, families, fitness and special interests. I'm imagining you either

a.) work full time
b.) work full time and are married or have a partner
c.) work full or part time, have a partner and one or more kids

However, if you've been really curious and daydreaming about being an entrepreneur, then the time is right to put more thought and energy behind that dream.

I want you to think BIG, no holding back, literally aim for the stars with your ideas. This first activity is straightforward and meant to get your creative juices flowing.

Write down three ideas you have for a business. If you have more than three, I encourage you not to exceed five because in the end you can only chose one to start with and the fewer choices upfront, the easier it will be to make a decision. You will come to find this whole path is comprised of making a lot of decisions along the way and that is also an aspect of leadership, making decisions sometimes daily and even multiple times a day.

If you're a person who likes to brainstorm a bit before committing anything in writing to your workbook pages, write your ideas on anything available: a Post-It note, napkin, anything you want, go for it. For example, when I was planning my business I used a white board and wrote down **all** my ideas and then started writing why I liked the ideas. Next I started writing down pros and cons for each idea – that is how brainstorming works, there is no wrong answer, whatever comes to mind you allow the thoughts to flow. When you are ready, record your ideas below.

YOUR IDEAS

1. _____

2. _____

3. _____

If you have never thought about starting a business before and that first step was challenging for you, the next step may come more easily. Next list three skills you possess. Everyone has skills. Be honest with yourself. For example, I have strong interpersonal skills that developed at a young age due to my work in the theater arts which also support my public speaking skills. When I was considering various business ideas, I knew giving presentations of some kind to women would be integrated into the business. When I finalized my concept and decided to launch with an online course and workbook, it felt like the right combination and balance of my skills, strengths and interests. List skills you are proud of and the ones in which you excel.

YOUR SKILLS

1. _____

2. _____

3. _____

Then to further build on the theme of you being comprised of a multitude of layers and elements that could contribute to your business idea, add three of your strengths below. This can provide further insight and possibly enhance one of the business ideas or highlight a personal skill you listed above. If you are not sure what your strengths are, you can ask someone close to you and that you trust or better yet, spend some time figuring this out.

One system that helps people identify their strengths is StrengthsFinder 2.0 recently rebranded as CliftonStrengths (see Resources Section.) There is a website and a book that I highly recommend you become familiar with. Like skills, everyone has strengths as well and the sooner you are familiar with your strengths, the sooner you can use them to help propel your business idea forward.

Strengths can include talents, knowledge and abilities. They are things that come easily to you or feel innate. For example, one of my strengths is "futuristic" and it manifests in a variety of ways however I recognize it because my tendency to is look ahead and imagine the possibilities. It's not something I force myself to do but rather this is my natural approach in work and life.

YOUR STRENGTHS (refer to CliftonStrengths 34 Themes)

1. _____

2. _____

3. _____

The final step to this initial ideation stage is to identify three areas of interest or activity you thoroughly enjoy doing and have done for at least one year. These can also help inform your business idea. Feel free to include any interests such as fitness, food, reading, music, volunteering or any hobbies. Basically anything you find yourself choosing to do when you have free time and that you find yourself losing track of time because it brings you so much joy that you could continue to do it if there were no time constraints.

YOUR INTERESTS

1. _____

2. _____

3. _____

Now, take a moment and go back through each step, paying close attention to what you wrote. These are all ideas and possibilities in which you could create some kind of new business. This is exciting stuff! Are there particular ideas that are more appealing than others, or stand out in some extraordinary way? Or are there any common themes?

Are there ones that you keep re-reading or invoke more excitement than the others? Go with that gut feeling. It is a manifestation of your passion and we don't always recognize it if we have been removed from truly and deeply experiencing our instinctual feelings. Passion persuades, and passion can keep you motivated throughout the entrepreneurial journey, as well as, inspire others around you.

Below is the first opportunity to make your own decision and it's an exercise in holding yourself accountable. Don't overthink it or you will delay making strides to reach your career freedom. There is no better time than the present. Make each moment count and know you have something special to offer the world. This is the first step.

Your first mission begins – you have 24 to 48 hours to confirm your idea.

My #1 Business Idea: _____

Activity 1.2

Entrepreneurship

What is an entrepreneur? Feel free to write down your definition in the space below and if you're not sure how to define entrepreneurship, search the term in any browser of choice.

A point to consider before you conduct your research is that entrepreneurs come in all shapes and sizes and you may be conjuring up an image of Sara Blakely (founder of Spanx, American billionaire businesswoman.) What unites entrepreneurs regardless of the size of their companies or the industries in which they serve is a common trait to create something for themselves, that solves a problem or enhances life. It is a unique idea coupled with a highly motivated internal drive to reach a goal. Several women entrepreneurs I know don't consider themselves entrepreneurs because they envision something big, someone they read about in the news, however they only need to remember *why* they started their own business to rekindle their entrepreneurial spirit.

What did you find?

What do you think about that definition? Are you open and willing to explore being one yourself? If you are, continue on!

If you are up for the challenge, go back to a browser and search for women entrepreneurs. Hopefully you will see pages of results. Depending on what you find, you could literally spend hours reading about women entrepreneurs across time, location and specialty. It's important to know of other women entrepreneurs so you know that this can be done and women are deciding to start their own businesses every day of the week, all around the world and have done so for years!

Now select three of those women entrepreneurs you read about and that are of particular interest to you. Record their names and what they founded below. Include a couple details that resonate with you.

Woman Entrepreneur 1

Name:

Founder of:

Details:

Woman Entrepreneur 2

Name:

Founder of:

Details:

Woman Entrepreneur 3

Name:

Founder of:

Details:

The first time I went through this exercise I was literally blown away with all the brilliance I was reading about, and I found the information alone to be inspiring. Stay on this path of inspiration. Keep searching for women who have succeeded on the entrepreneurial path. The below exercise is similar to the above exercise; however, this time enter the same search terms "women entrepreneurs" and include "videos." You could also go to a channel such as YouTube and conduct this search.

Select 1-3 to watch. In the space below, note what stood out to you. Were there any themes that spoke to you or inspired you?

Woman Entrepreneur(s) Videos

Name(s):

_____

Inspired by:

You've worked halfway through the first module. You've vetted initial ideas as well as researched entrepreneurship and specifically women entrepreneurs. If your interest in forming your own business continues, then you'll want to work through the last two activities for this module.

In addition to cultivating your own skills, strengths, insights and emotional intelligence to stay on this adventurous path, you will need others around you. It can be an exhilarating ride or a bumpy ride, nonetheless it's important to be able to connect with others, share stories and at times seek support.

Activity 1.3

Personal Advisory Team

Most likely there are people you go to for certain aspects of your life whether you are seeking their input, feedback, encouragement and at times perhaps even those people you know who will challenge your ideas and opinions. You need all of these perspectives. There may be one or more go-to persons in your life; appreciate their insight and wisdom and listen to their feedback. Expanding this resource will be useful in meeting your entrepreneurial challenges.

This approach of identifying a few go-to people allows for diversity among your support group and will validate that other people **do** want to see you succeed. There are two lessons for forming this group. One lesson is simply a mental acknowledgement to yourself about who these people are and you may choose to keep it to yourself that they are your personal advisors, OR you may want to formally tell people you are starting your own business and want a personal advisory team to help you trouble shoot through challenges as they arise and you've identified them as one of those people you'd like on your team.

Below is a list of topics. Next to each topic write the name of the person or people who you consider as a trusted resource for discussing your business idea(s). In addition, add more topics relevant to you or areas in which you know you will need additional support. This can include specific business skills or areas that are more about personal development and growth.

Financials

_____

Social Media

_____

Website

_____

Product/Service Feedback

_____

Wellness

_____

Networking Events

_____

Professional Development Opportunities

_____

Social/Cultural Ideas

_____

Fitness

_____

Other

_____

Other

_____

Other

_____

Take a look at your list. Did you end up writing the same person's name more than once? If so, that is definitely someone you will want in your Personal Advisory Team.

On the flip side, did you list someone different for every topic? If so, consider how much access you have to that person and if he/she will be there in your greatest times of need. If you have anyone in your list that is hard to reach, get a hold of, has trouble returning calls or due to time zone difference you just can't seem to connect when you want to, you probably need to consider someone else. It may prove too difficult if you want to lean into them while forming your business and relating to you on the many and various aspects in which you will need support in upcoming weeks and months.

I encourage you to not go overboard and keep your Personal Advisory Team relatively small, literally three to five people.

If you choose to tell these individuals you're forming a Personal Advisory Team and that you have identified them as potential members of that group, be sure to confirm their interest. You may want to let them know exactly what that means from a commitment perspective. It may translate as no change whatsoever to the current relationship, or you may be seeking them out more than usual or desire a more frequent link up, perhaps starting with once a month. If you ask people to do this, let them know what it means to you.

These individuals are key to your success so be sure to thank them along the way. Everyone needs support and you will find at times if your focus weakens or life throws you some curve balls, they will help you stay the course. They are a fundamental and integral part of your network.

Form a Personal Advisory Team.

My deadline for forming a Personal Advisory Team is (enter a date):

In addition to an advisory group, it's important to have peers you can relate with throughout the journey as well. Below is the final activity for this module.

Activity 1.4

Peer Groups

Peer groups and community groups are as equally important as forming a personal advisory team, especially if you are a solopreneur and working from home. We all need other people to share ideas with or bounce ideas off of, to receive feedback, to help us troubleshoot and in general to connect with **likeminded people**. Some friends and family members may not understand or be risk adverse and unconsciously discourage you from taking the leap. When you start your own business, you are not alone – people do this every day and it truly helps to have other people going through some of the same things you are to discuss the experience. It also helps to have people who can assist you in staying the course.

Having friends and professional peers around you who have started their own businesses and being part of networks of entrepreneurs, will help you stay on your path.

If you happen to live in a place that you are unaware of entrepreneurial networks, all you have to do is search "meetups" and search the categories, or search for 1 Million Cups, an initiative sponsored by the Kauffman Foundation. LinkedIn is a useful tool where you can search for people, confirm who is already part of your network, and identify your first degree contacts as well as notice second degree connections you would like to pursue.

If you don't have either of these options, perhaps you are the person who needs to start one in your community!

Search for entrepreneurial networks, events, meetups or "events for women entrepreneurs." You may wish to add "in a location near me." Below list three of these groups or events:

1. _____

2. _____

3. _____

If you live in a place where it would take you too much time to get to that location or you literally can't see yourself spearheading such an initiative with everything else you have to juggle, form a small peer group in your town. Go out for coffee or drinks once a month; make it simple and easy for everyone. You only need an hour. Just be sure it is a group of people who run or are starting their own businesses.

One more possibility depending on your circumstances is to start a virtual group. You could try Google Hangouts/Meetup, Skype, Slack conversations and there are all kinds of video conferencing tools available from GoToMeeting, JoinMe, ReadyTalk, Zoom, etc. – many come with a price tag however most offer a 30day free trial so perhaps if you try a weekly virtual meetup, you'll find it's worth the investment. You can join Zoom for free forever as long as the meetings are less than 40 minutes. Start with free tools whenever possible.

Find at least one local entrepreneurial event to attend on a regular basis. Add the event to your calendar and plan to attend within the next 30 days.

This is part of the entrepreneurial ecosystem and may very well be the key to keeping you on course when others around you may abandon ship. You may be surprised how those closest to you don't fully understand or appreciate the challenges of this new journey in which you are embarking upon. It can be disheartening and know this is normal for women entrepreneurs to encounter. Stay the course, lean into like-minded others and don't go it alone.

Intentionally left blank

MODULE 2
BUILD YOUR LAUNCHPAD

"I was smart enough to go through any door that opened."

- Joan Rivers

You have to slow down in order to speed up for certain things to come to fruition. In order to start a business you are presenting a solution to a problem. You may have a great idea; however, you need to discover what will sell and therefore need to conduct customer research – that is what this module is about. New companies are starting every day and unfortunately the odds are nine out of ten businesses fail, it's a disheartening statistic. One of the reasons this happens is people spend their own money on something without validating the market need, otherwise known as market validation.

Building a business is a lot of work however it can progress by taking small steps each day. Have you thought about a consistent time each day you can dedicate to cultivating your business idea? Or, have you created a varied schedule for yourself? It may be a different time each day; however, you need to note somehow when you will put time and energy into your endeavor. If not, I encourage you to put this workbook down right now and take a look at your calendar.

Search for available timeslots and block them off. Do not schedule other events over this dedicated time and if someone asks you to do something, you will need to be fully committed to yourself and cultivating your business idea. You are busy and can look for other available options. Print out your weekly calendar if you aren't in the habit of checking an electronic calendar or if you want a more prominent, visual reminder. Include weekly reminders for activities, tasks and milestones to achieve. At the end of each week, acknowledge what you have accomplished.

> **Find a consistent 30 to 60 minutes daily, and book it on your calendar. Remain flexible about the time of day if your calendar is busy, however strive to find a consistent daily time to cultivate your business idea.**
> **What's most important is that you find time to do something every day to move your business forward. (You may enjoy the consistency of the routine once it is established!)**

 **Objectives:**

As a result of completing the activities in this module you will be able to:

- **Finalize the offering of your company**
- **Identify next preparation steps and supplies needed**
- **Understand the LaunchPad Blueprint**
- **Establish components of the Marketing Research Navigation Map (learn how to conduct market research!)**
- **Learn how to create and conduct a survey**
- **Create customer personas**

Once you have reserved time for yourself, create a preparation checklist. Consider things you may need or already have or conversations you need to pursue. Below are a few examples to start you off.

Activity 2.1

Preparation Checklist

In the table below create a list of activities you need to complete before you are ready to launch your business. This can include long term activities however you will want to focus on activities that can be accomplished in the short term so that you continue to take steps each day, week and month to move your business forward. Some activities may be ongoing activities such as scheduling time to work on your business every day; however, this initial "to-do" list is an effort to keep your business plan on course.

Activity
e.g. Schedule daily time to build the business
Research types of business entities
Look for good deals on supplies and equipment
Discuss business idea with family members

Activity 2.2

Your Company Questionnaire

Below is another activity to get you thinking through your business idea. It's a short questionnaire to further flesh out the idea you landed on to pursue. Keep your responses concise. If you were to stand up and read this to someone, the information should be delivered within 5 minutes. If you don't have someone to read it to, read it out loud in front of a mirror.

1. What is your company name?

2. What story can you tell about what you are offering?

3. Revisit product ideas. What is/are your product(s) or service(s)?

4. Who is your key customer in general (age, gender, demographics - more detailed activity in following module)?

5. What is your brand (fun, quirky, intelligent, sporty, friendly, creative, natural)? If your product/company was a person, what would it be like?

6. What colors represent your brand well?

You will want to strive for consistency across business email, social media channels and your website to establish a strong brand identity.

Additional Question

7. What is your preferred website name url? If that url is not available, what are other variations?

At this stage the above question is meant to record your initial ideas about your website domain name. In a later module there is an activity to conduct a search for domain names and registration.

Many people prefer a more visual way to work through ideas. Visuals are fantastic, especially when they accurately represent a concept, activities, steps or stages. A way to further work through the above questions is to fill out the Launchpad Blueprint provided on the next page. The inspiration for the Launchpad Blueprint came from the Lean Business Canvas Model and the Business Canvas Model. Several ideas and concepts can be worked through with a one-pager versus a 30 - page traditional business plan. (If you decide to be a hi-tech company seeking venture capital - other people's money, then you will need to work on a more detailed business plan.) If you want to learn more about the Business Canvas model, follow this link:

http://diytoolkit.org/tools/business-model-canvas/

Activity 2.3

The Launchpad Blueprint

Work your way through each section below, filling in your initial responses. You may fine tune your responses over time. Short examples are provided; however, if you prefer a blank version, this can be found in the Resources section at the end of this book.

What (Product/ Service)	Who (Customer Personas)	How (Market Channels)	Where (Store, Online)
e.g. Online Courses	e.g. Working Moms	e.g. Social media, email & blog	e.g. Online

Differentiator (Competitive Advantage)	Expenses (Costs of Supplies)	Competitors (Name 2-3)	Pricing (The cost)
e.g. Experience from all sides of entrepreneurship	e.g. Video camera - $1,000	e.g. Udemy, Lynda.com & Teachable	e.g. Under $300 per course

Activity 2.4

Market Research Navigation Map

Before you fully pursue your plan, it's important to know what the competition is doing, and it may very well enhance your thinking. You will want to learn as much as you can, and a lot of information can be gleaned from the internet alone. Notice how competitors message what they are doing and pay close attention if any pricing information is available online. Also observe what social media channels they use.

The competitive landscape is important to know; however, be aware when you start researching it is easy to go down a rabbit hole. Rabbit holes can distract you from your main goal and could thwart your progress. Plan on spending thirty minutes on your initial competitors' analysis and then check in to see what you have discovered. If you are two steps removed from your competitor's site and reviewing other topics, you've gone down a rabbit hole!

Below is a tool that will walk you through creating a Market Research Navigation Map based on the competitor analysis you conduct. Give yourself some time to complete this activity; it could take a few hours or more to thoroughly explore the competitive landscape.

See next page.

Tool: Market Research Navigation Map		Your Business Name:	
Name of Competitor 1:	**Uniqueness or Challenges this business faces**	**Name of Competitor 2:**	**Uniqueness or Challenges this business faces**
How are they marketing?	Strengths	How are they marketing?	Strengths
What type of product/service do they sell?		What type of product/service do they sell?	
	Weaknesses		Weaknesses
What is the price?		What is the price?	

Pricing Strategy for Your Business

Goals & Objectives (inexpensive, affordable, rare and one of a kind, etc.)	**Growth Opportunities & Ideas**	**Current Challenges & Needs**

What is the price and why?	Other options and pricing to give you a competitive advantage?	Any known weaknesses or threats?

Once this is completed you will know a lot more than when you began forming your business idea. Items you will want to consider in weeks ahead are those elements that differentiate you from your competitors. What can you do better? How will your pricing compare and what is the goal with your pricing rationale? You could be the top of the line, highest quality option or the most economical option, it depends on who you are targeting. In regard to pricing alone, you may have to experiment a bit. I know business owners who do this all the time because they are *listening* to their customers and you may find yourself in an unusually competitive environment.

> **Listen to your customers and you will not only improve your business offerings, you will gain customer loyalty. Listening is the secret sauce to business success.**

Activity 2.5

Conduct a Survey

Conduct a quick online survey with family, friends, and peers to solicit interest and feedback. Keep the survey as short as possible and let participants know how much of their time it will take. The very first survey you conduct may be longer than ones you will conduct in the future – this one is your first attempt to collect real world market data and you want to optimize the results.

If you really aren't sure of who would want your product or services or can only identify one customer persona, conduct a survey. To create your list of recipients first consider your own network comprised of family, friends, colleagues and community members. If you need more people, then consider your social media networks, neighbors or you can ask the people on your initial list to send the survey to three people they know.

Currently there are many free tools available at the writing of this workbook such as Survey Monkey.

https://www.surveymonkey.com/

If you are not sure where your customer shops or the level of interest in your product or service, conducting a survey can be incredibly insightful. If you are using Google's G Suite it includes Google Forms which are a simple, easy way to create a survey and have the results sent straight to your inbox. In case you are unfamiliar with G Suite it was formerly known as Google Apps and includes Gmail (email client), Docs (akin to Microsoft Word or Mac Pages), Drive (storage space) and Calendar all for your business needs. Personally I like how seamlessly integrated the tools are and that they can be accessed from a computer or a phone. At the time of publishing the first edition of this workbook G Suite is only $5 per month for one user.

You will want to dedicate some time to collect information and test your assumptions. Observe the responses and see who is favorable to your business idea. Consider including an opinion question where the respondent can agree or disagree by varying levels. Down the road you may choose to obtain feedback from your clients during certain times of the year and you could use a Net Promotor Score (NPS) to understand their satisfaction. It may be someone already in your personal network who you would be able to write out the persona details easily. If the survey is shared with your contacts' network, it may be there is another persona out there unbeknownst to you that is highly interested in your product or service.

3 Tips to a Create a User Friendly Survey

- Limit your survey to five questions and indicate how much time it will take to fill out. (i.e. This will take less than 5 minutes.)

- Use a multiple choice format whenever possible. This ensures the time indicated above remains true. List the most positive/best answer first since we read from left to right.

- Always end your survey with an open-ended question. This gives your potential customers an opportunity to share information with you freely and possibly confirm where personal interest and affinity connections exist.

Sample Survey Questions

1. Where do you currently buy _____?
   a) local business
   b) shopping mall
   c) online
   d) other

2. On average, how much do you pay for this? (include dollar amounts in ranges)
   a) $1 - 5
   b) $5 -10
   c) $10 -15
   d) $15 or more

3. What are your go to resources to find more or other variety of _____? (create a multiple choice response)

4. What channels do you or would you use to find out more information about _____? (create a checklist similar to below and allow respondents to check all that apply)
   a) social media channels
   b) internet sites
   c) direct mail such as postcards, fliers, etc.
   d) radio

5. What else would you like me to know or think I should consider before starting this particular business?

Knowing your customers is one of the greatest strengths you can have when building a business, maintaining that business and possibly one day scaling that business. Your loyal customers will help see to that and they will become your best marketing channel. When people "sell" your product or services for you, selling efforts become much easier. Selling is about conversations that result in a transaction.

On the next page is an example of a real survey I sent in the early stages of forming my company. It was an insightful exercise to go through since I know a lot of women entrepreneurs across industries to include hi-tech, the arts and wellness. Among the recipients were women who worked full time for themselves, part time for themselves and some were straddling jobs at a company while trying to get their own businesses off the ground. The demographical age range was between late twenties and late forties, some being mothers, while others were single. Based on their responses I was able to conclude that my approach to starting your own company works well for entrepreneurial moms. It can be a challenge to find daily time to dedicate to cultivating your business when there are so many other responsibilities to juggle, however taking small incremental steps each day will produce results!

Survey Example

1. Would you take (or would you have taken) an online course to learn how to build your business?
   Yes / No / Maybe

2. How much time per week could you commit to learning these skills?

   30 minutes / 45 minutes / 1 hour / 1.5 hours / 2 hours / Other

3. How much would you be willing to pay for a two hour online course that includes 10 hours of real world applied business skills and knowledge?

   $25 / $35 / $50 / $75 / $95 / Other

4. What channels would you search for this type of information (check all that apply):
   - Web search
   - Udemy
   - Kahn academy
   - Lynda.com
   - Etsy
   - Pinterest
   - Facebook
   - LinkedIn
   - Twitter
   - Instagram
   - Blogs
   - Fliers
   - Other

5. What would you like me to know or think I should consider for building a business to provide resources for women entrepreneurs? (Long answer text)

Create a survey and send it to a minimum of 15 people and no more than 50 people within the next week.

Depending on the tool you use to create the survey, you will be able to see responses and most likely compiled results. After a week passes by, you can re-send to those who didn't respond the first time, trying to elicit a few more responses.

Activity 2.6

Customer Personas

The first step is to attract the right customer personas and get the conversation started. You will need to demonstrate what problem you are solving, how are you addressing their pain points? Is your product or service easily accessible at the places they shop and is it in their budget? The other aspect of selling is appealing to the psychology of the consumer. Many products and services on the market these days appeal to the senses, quality of life or are for entertainment.

Think through the various types of people who would use your product or services. When we get to the marketing section there will be more time spent on messaging to certain customer personas and which channels work best; however, for now identifying main traits will work to keep moving your idea forward. Be as specific as possible.

Write three customer personas. If you are not sure who your exact customer is yet, skip over the area below to "Conduct a Survey" and then come back to this after your survey has concluded. You can search for free stock photos of the "perfect" person for your various customer personas to truly visualize who you are targeting with your communications.

Persona #1

Name: _____

Age: _____

Occupation: _____

Education Level: _____

Relationship Status: _____

Hobbies/ Interests:

Where this persona shops or spends money:

What social media do they use?

Persona #2

Name: _____

Age: _____

Occupation: _____

Education Level: _____

Relationship Status: _____

Hobbies/ Interests:

Where this persona shops or spends money:

What social media do they use?

Persona #3

Name: _____

Age: ____

Occupation: _____

Education Level: _____

Relationship Status: _____

Hobbies/ Interests:

Where this persona shops or spends money:

What social media do they use?

Intentionally left blank

MODULE 3
COMMAND CENTER

"Knowing what must be done does away with fear."

- Rosa Parks

Now that you are clear on your customer personas, you will want to be clear about your product or service. Do you have initial costs to consider? Not only items such as a laptop or work space but do you need supplies to build your product? Make a list of what you need for your business venture and research the costs. It may be that you already have what you need or that you can get away with little to no investment in the early days; however, it all depends on what you're planning to sell. It is helpful to create a workspace for yourself even if it's a small section of a room if you don't have an office space of your own. If you need to be able to setup and take down your "work space" quickly and easily, create your own office-in-a-box containing the essentials you need.

It can be easy to get caught up in the dream of FINALLY doing your own thing and wanting a fresh start, with all new bright and shiny objects. Please don't waste your money on non-essential items. Use everything you can that you already own and then search for the best deal on supplies. Searching on the internet will give you great insight into the cost of your idea and how you will need to prepare financially to take the plunge. Be sure to check out a few sites to compare pricing and to stay informed. I am a huge believer in bootstrapping which means you will not take money from others in the very early stages and that you will be scrappy and keep things as low cost as possible. Strive to keep your costs low and the quality of your product or service high.

Objectives:

As a result of completing the activities in this module you will be able to:

- **Further refine your business idea**
- **Start design and content considerations for your website**
- **Secure and register your domain**
- **Understand the basics of SEO**
- **Define your marketing strategy**
- **Create your brand**

Activity 3.1

Website Assessment

To identify the type of site you want to have, begin by exploring your favorite websites. Notice what appeals to you and which design elements you could incorporate for yourself. What about them draws you in and keeps you coming back? Is it the visual layout, the content, ease of navigation or all of the above? The activity below encourages you to select your top three websites and to note what exactly you liked about the sites. First step: search for your favorite site and be thinking of two more. Note the details of what you find below.

Site 1

1) Website address:

2) Navigation orientation (circle one) - horizontal or vertical

3) List tab labels (Examples: About, Home, Services):

4) Number of pages (indicated by number of tabs and any drop down selection beneath each tab):

5) Primary colors used throughout the site:

6) Images (circle one) – yes or no

7) Videos (circle one) – yes or no

8) What was most striking?

9) Call to Actions (CTA) – buttons to click on to download interesting information or enter your email to join an event, be added to a mailing list.

10) Messaging

11) Tone (i.e. serious, witty, playful):

Site 2

1) Website address:

2) Navigation orientation (circle one) - horizontal or vertical

3) List tab labels (Examples: About, Home, Services):

4) Number of pages (indicated by number of tabs and any drop down selection beneath each tab):

5) Primary colors used throughout the site:

6) Images (circle one) – yes or no

7) Videos (circle one) – yes or no

8) What was most striking?

9) Call to Actions (CTA) – buttons to click on to download interesting information or entering your email to join an event or be added to a mailing list.

10) Messaging

11) Tone (i.e. serious, witty, playful):
Site 3

1) Website address:

2) Navigation orientation (circle one) - horizontal or vertical

3) List tab labels (Examples: About, Home, Services):

4) Number of pages (indicated by number of tabs and any drop down selection beneath each tab):

5) Primary colors used throughout the site:

6) Images (circle one) – yes or no

7) Videos (circle one) – yes or no

8) What was most striking?

9) Call to Actions (CTA) – buttons to click on to download interesting information or entering your email to join an event, be added to a mailing list.

10) Messaging

11) Tone (i.e. serious, witty, playful):

Once you have gone through this activity you will have a sense of the tone and other elements to capture on your website. A few years back I remember there being a rumor among marketing circles that email and websites were going to die. Although there is a decline in email usage with some generations (they text, why would they need email?) for certain generations email is well received. This type of preference is important to know about your customer profile demographics. Things change over time however your key customer profile may stay intact for some years.

Activity 3.2

Domain Search & Registration

You will want to be consistent with your brand and a simple way to achieve this is to have items such as your email address match the naming schema of your website. One simple way to make sure this is streamlined is to setup a Google G Suite (referenced in Module 2, Activity 2.5) email account which will prompt you to secure your business domain name.

1. Go to G Suite, setup your business email and indicate you need a domain. Enter your preferred domain name, click on Search Domain (or do this through a domain company.)

2. Confirm ".com" is available and affordable. If not try .org, .net, .biz. If none are available, you will need to get creative and come up with another name variation. It can be helpful to recruit a trusted friend to help you brainstorm the names or lean in to your peer group.

3. Create an account and record your login credentials.

4. Enter the credit card information to secure your domain name.

Note: Later you will create a website and eventually follow the steps for publishing it. Your website building tool as well, as the company in which you purchase the domain (sometimes these are the same company), have staff who can help you with the final stages of publishing your site. Publishing is an action that can take some hours before it is live, in some cases it is rather immediate.

As we explore website building options and tips, some topics are considered more advanced. My goal with this workbook is to expose you to the variety of activities and skills you need to consider when starting your own business. By no means do you need to be an expert at everything; however, a little knowledge can go a long way.

One such topic considered more advanced is Search Engine Optimization (SEO) and you will want to keep it in mind as you build your site. SEO is about designing your site and promoting it so that search engines know how to categorize it and show it in search results. The goal is to get your site to be listed near the top of search results when the product or service you are selling is searched for so that potential customers look at your site first. You want people to find you!

If this topic overwhelms you or is intimidating to you, set it aside for now, and revisit it in six months. Once you have accomplished various aspects of getting your company off the ground, you will be able to apply and build additional business skills and knowledge.

5 Easy to Implement SEO Tips

1. Monitor Your Website Activity

Set up Google Analytics for your website – it's free! This allows you to track your visitors activity on your site including what pages they visit, how long they stay, how many times they've visited (for example during a week,) where they are located and the search terms they entered to find your site.

2. Use Keywords

Search engines categorize pages using the keywords found on a webpage. Search engines will look at the webpage title and the content on that page. Then when a search is conducted it will pull up the webpages whose keywords correspond with the search. You need to have content on your webpage that uses the words of items you sell and any of its synonyms so that search engines can easily categorize your page. Some website builders literally include categories for each page to include: Page Title, Page Description and Meta Keywords. These categories are all appear in search engines.

3. Link Back

This simply means that if you ever write a blog about a certain subject matter or specialty area and someone decides to post your blog on their website, make sure that in your blog you mention your website where readers can go to buy goods and services from you. Search engines will pick up that someone else's website mentions your website and this will give your site more credit in the search engines' eyes.

4. Keep Content Fresh

Search engines pick up on when a site has added new content to its pages and this will help your website get closer to the top of searches.

5. Link to Others

Develop relationships with other sites in hopes that they will add a link to your site on their site. This is also referred to as co-marketing a type of partnership you can pitch to people if you want to pursue some low touch business partnerships.

Speaking of relationships, we will explore the importance and power of your network in the next module. The are many ways in which your network will work for you and it's important to segment the people in your network so that your communications are effective. Keep going. You're half the way ready for takeoff!

In regard to a website, currently there are a handful of free options available in which you can choose a template and literally drag and drop the elements you want on your website. It couldn't be easier for those of us with no formal background in design. Most of these companies include tutorial resources and can help you understand balancing elements on a page to include images, space bars and text.

The best way to learn how to set up a website is to just do it. Take the leap!

It won't be live to the world until you publish it, so don't worry if it's not perfect at the beginning. In addition, you will want to periodically update your website, so you will always have an opportunity to make changes. To get started you need to map out what pages you need on your site, navigation preference and then you will determine the content for each page. Remember less is more, so if you find yourself writing several paragraphs it most likely is information overload or you can simply guide people to other pages by inserting "learn more" and link to the relevant information. Focus on the essentials and what will draw people in.

First determine the pages you want on your site. Below is a short list to consider:

- About
- Product/Services
- Pricing/ Order Now
- Team
- Contact

In the early stages you may keep it as simple as that or you may keep those header sections general and then have pages within each category. Sometimes people will include History or Team Bios or Board Members under the About section. There are a lot of options; however, in order to not overwhelm yourself, keep it simple.

Purchase a domain name, determine website menu structure and start building your website content within the next 48 hours.

Building a website can be done quickly however you do want it to reflect well on you and your business. Therefore you can start building the content and schedule on a calendar when you want to publish your website. You will want to update your website regularly; therefore you will always have an opportunity to edit or expand your site.

Several topics have been introduced and you're about halfway through this Module. Take a moment to confirm the items you need to consider for your website. You can check the items below once they are ready.

__ Domain name
__ Website menu structure
__ Pages and content
__ Images – logo, photos, icons
__ Website building tool
__ E-commerce tool if purchases can be made directly from your website (some website building tools offer e-commerce options)

Activity 3.3

The below activity was designed to walk you through forming your first strategic marketing plan. With each section below, write your response to each question. Take your time and if you don't know the answer right away, move onto the next question. Think through what you can manage in the early stages as well as your ideal scenario of how you will market your business. In time you could outsource marketing to a third party if this seems daunting to manage; however, thinking through these aspects will keep you informed and knowledgeable about how effective marketing can be.

Marketing Strategy Map

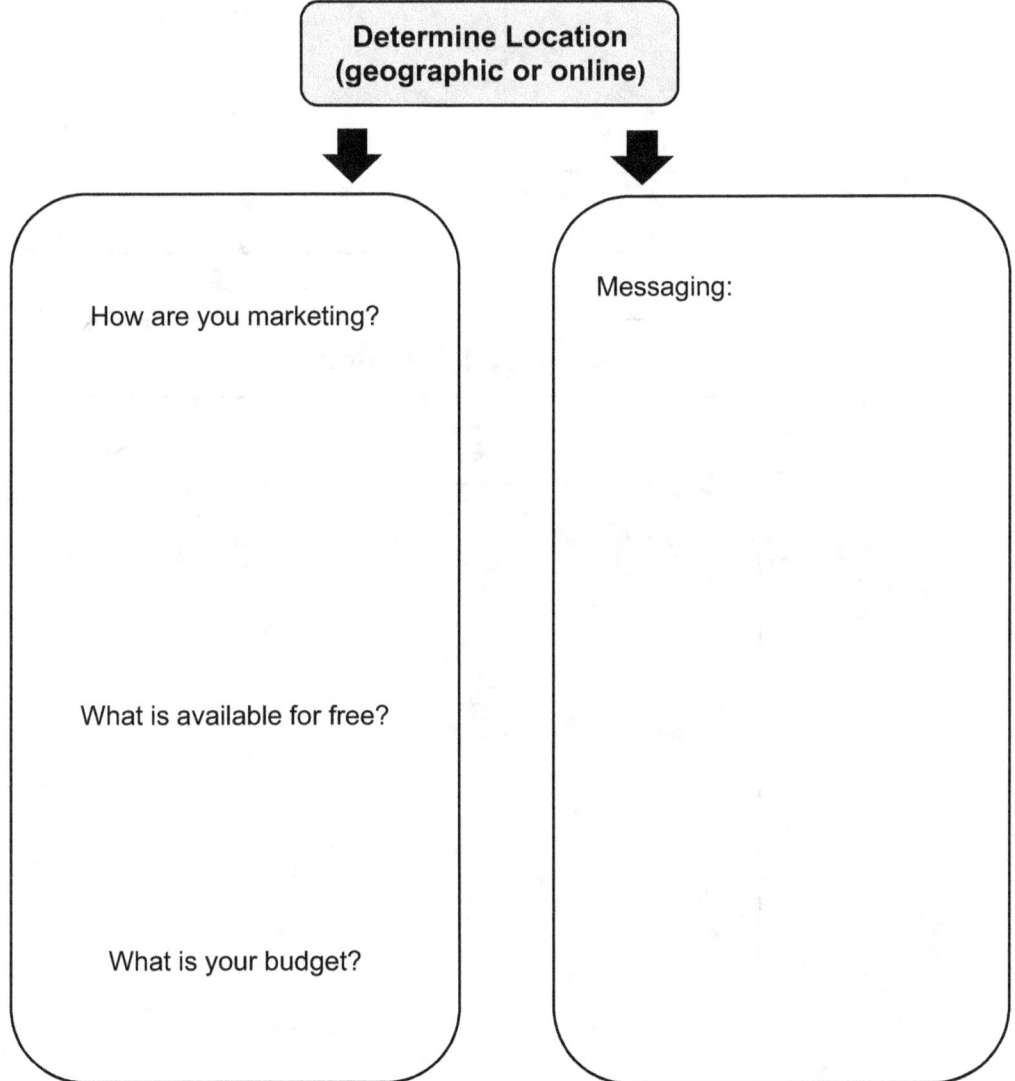

Determine Location
(geographic or online)

How are you marketing?

What is available for free?

What is your budget?

Messaging:

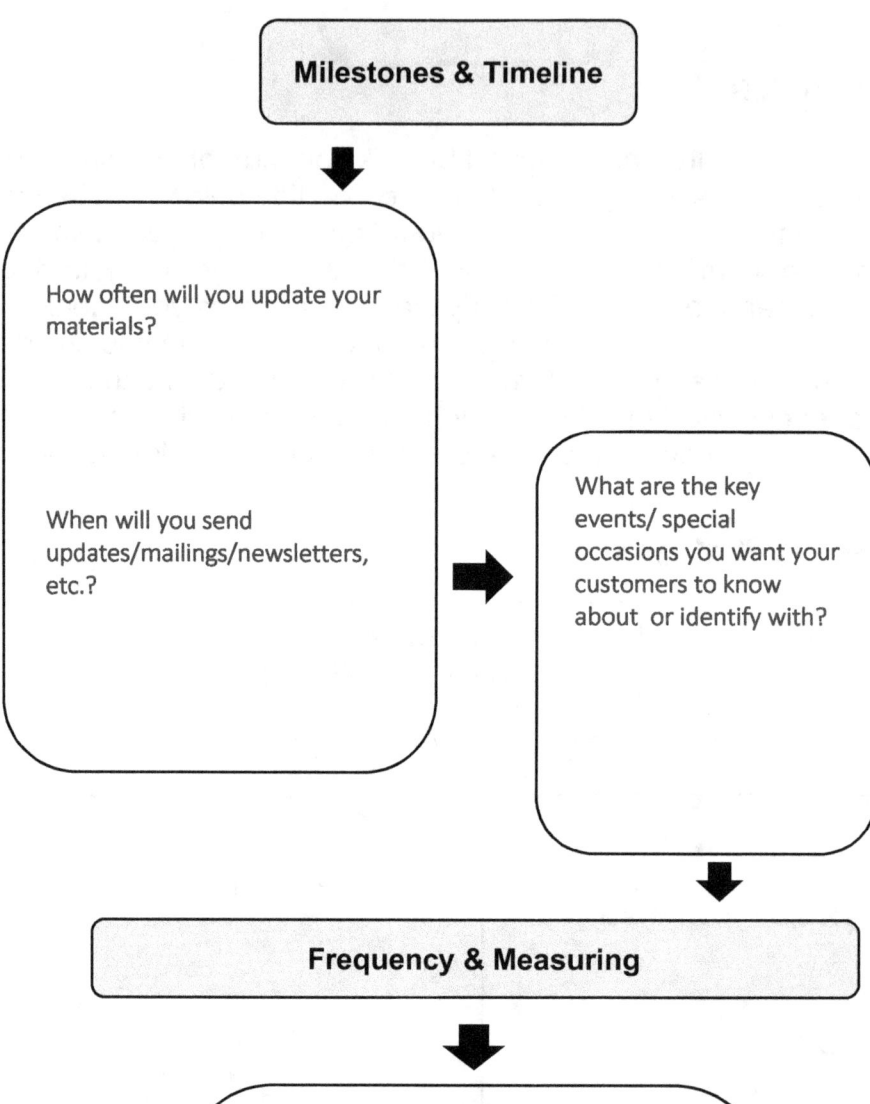

Milestones & Timeline

How often will you update your materials?

When will you send updates/mailings/newsletters, etc.?

What are the key events/ special occasions you want your customers to know about or identify with?

Frequency & Measuring

How often will you promote your product or service?

How will you measure your efforts to know they are producing the results you desire?

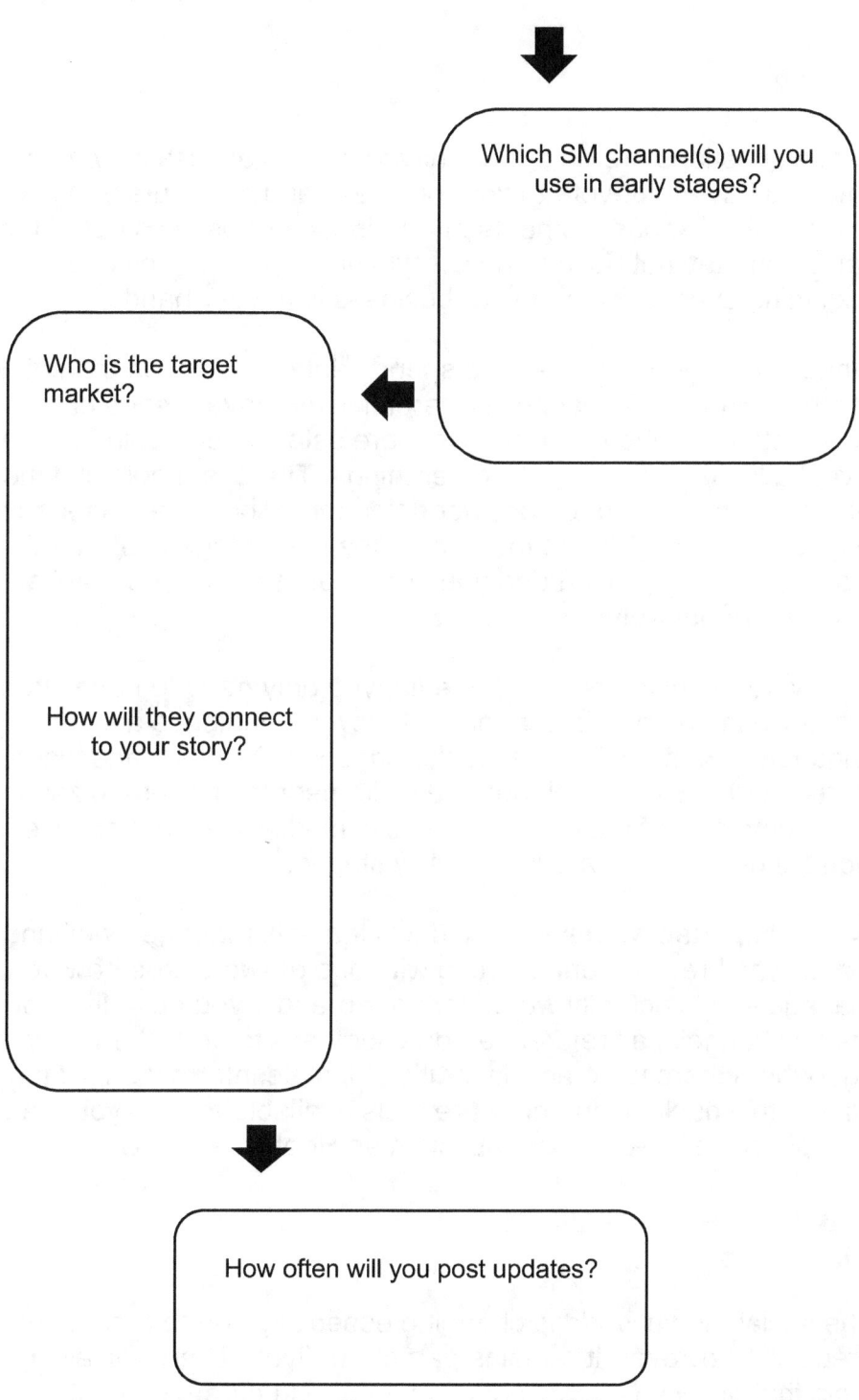

Social Media Strategy

Which SM channel(s) will you use in early stages?

Who is the target market?

How will they connect to your story?

How often will you post updates?

These questions are an opportunity for you to assess how much time you have to devote to your business and to ensure you can manage the various elements of running your business out of the gate. You may not have to do everything long-term; however, in the beginning every aspect of your business is in your hands.

Please know you don't have to spend a lot of money on marketing at the beginning. Be especially careful if you have friends or acquaintances who run their own more established businesses and invest a lot in advertising, or other things. There is a point in time where you may need to consider doing more, however it is a good way to see money fly out the door in the early stages before things really get off the ground and you don't want to blow your capital reserve prematurely.

One word of advice on social media, you only need to have strong presence in one or two channels to grow an audience and stay engaged with them. The key is the engagement piece and when starting out you can seek out and invite people and organizations to become part of your business social media network because they won't know who you are in the early stages.

What's important with social media is that it is managed well and that is why I recommend starting with one or two to see how you manage it. It is actually worse for your brand if you have five social media channels, all referenced on your website and when people go to them there is no activity or it's old, stale information. At the time of this publication, there are tools available to help you manage multiple social media accounts such as Hootsuite and Buffer.

https://hootsuite.com/platform
https://buffer.com/

The social media world is changing especially due to recent security breaches; however, it remains part of our lives. There will always be tools that allow you to schedule, monitor and curate content from one place.

Activity 3.4

Your Brand Solar System

I believe knowing your values is core to the journey you are embarking upon. By being an entrepreneur, you need to have a clear vision and be clear about your values.

> **Your values root you and influence all that you do, literally from the choices you make, to how you spend free time. Your values influence the people in which you choose to spend time.**
>
> **Values are powerful and they are core to your brand.**

For you to explore your business brand, I've created an aerial view of the solar system in which you can fill out and literally color it to your vision. There are some specific items I want you to work through so that you walk away with a decent understanding of what your brand represents. Use the map, the key and further instructions provided below. You will need some writing utensil in various colors to complete your brand solar system (pens, pencils, crayons, etc.)

KEY
- Values – the Sun
- Tone – 3 other planets
- Strengths – draw in the stars
- Weaknesses – Asteroid belt (draw a circle of asteroids, label them)
- Mental approach - Saturn
- Colors – orbital rings

See instructions below image.

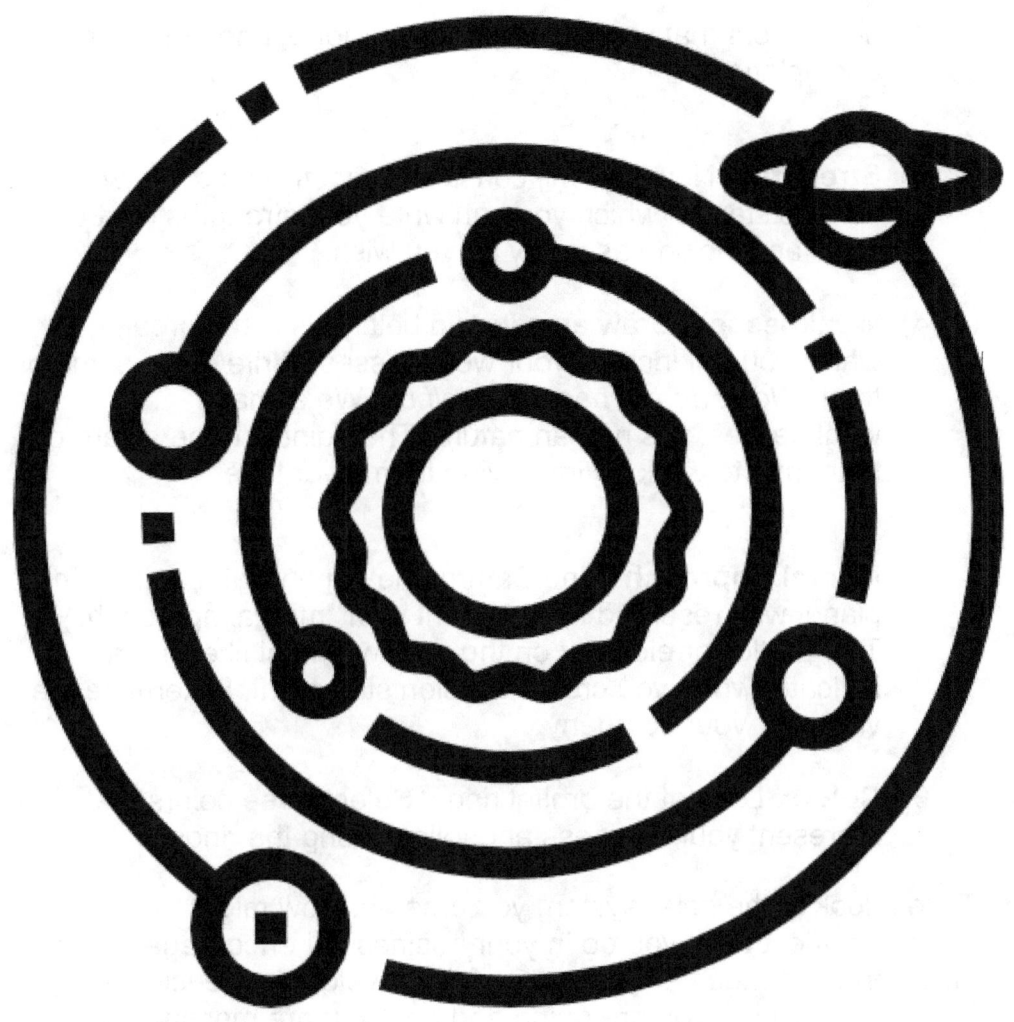

INSTRUCTIONS

1) **Values.** You're going to start at the core, with the Sun directly in the middle of the map. Please write in your top 3 values. If you run out of room, write to the side and draw a line to the sun.

2) **Tone.** Next you will consider the tone of your messaging. Is your business friendly, intelligent, whimsical, funny, serious, playful, etc.? Decide on the "tone" you want your business to have and remember all the marketing channels you will be using. Select a few planets (except Saturn) and write 3

descriptors that would comprise your tone, one descriptor in each planet.

3) **Strengths**. Now you will consider your strengths. Draw various stars in which you can write your strengths next to them and include as many as you wish.

4) **Weaknesses**. Draw an asteroid belt. This is the area in which you will include your weaknesses. Write down some of them. *Note: do not beat yourself up*. We all have weaknesses, it is human nature. The point is to be aware of them and to work on improving them over time.

5) **Mental Approach**. Find Saturn, the big one with a ring. This planet was reserved to represent your "mental approach." This particular element on the map will most likely be an indicator when you create a vision statement. Determine the vision for your company.

6) **Colors.** Look at the orbital rings. Select three colors that represent your business and follow along the rings.

Take a look at the solar system you created. How might these elements affect what you do in your business? I encourage you to incorporate as much as you can to fully develop your business brand so that what you are doing and how you are messaging resonates with you at a core level. I do realize there are times where one of the color that best represents you, or one of your favorite colors, may not be the right color for your business. That's OK! At least you are clear on how you as an individual, starting your own business like to represent yourself. This is part of image, self-awareness and colors in your environment all of which affect your perspective and in some cases your self - confidence.

If other colors represent your business better, use them. Akin to other activities in this guidebook, ask some friends, family or peers about items such as the colors that may best suit your business. They will tell you what they think – believe me, everyone has an opinion and people are delighted to share their thoughts, so ask them to confirm and further validate. You can even conduct a poll and I have found this is helpful when viewing logo designs. Let people vote and read their feedback!

Your Brand Solar System can serve as a template for creating, composing and informing your marketing communications. This is a powerful tool and worth posting so that it is a visible, daily reminder of what you stand for and what you are building. You can always go back to it, or refer to it any time to see if something you want to message out aligns with your brand identity. You may find the above activity incredibly easy or incredibly difficult, based on experience people tend to fall in one of two extremes.

In fact, you can take your time with the above activity and reflect on each of the elements to capture what you really want to evoke with your brand. Even after going through the activity, a few days later you may wish to change something. It's funny how certain words can strike you in a moment or how analytical we can become about the impact of a word when given a limited range in which to *represent ourselves and our business.*

The only thing I would advise against is publicly changing your vision, values or colors on a monthly or quarterly basis. It's not a bad habit to regularly review to see if the values are being upheld, however if you publicly and frequently change your messaging and brand you will appear unstable, unpredictable and that clearly sends a negative impression to your current client base and some potential future customers.

Intentionally left blank

MODULE 4
WHAT THE NUMBERS TELL YOU

"I didn't get there by wishing for it or hoping for it, but by working for it."

- Estée Lauder

There are two main themes I want you to keep in mind when it comes to your business financials:

1. Numbers tell a story – your financials will tell the story of your company through numbers.
2. Money is a resource – learn how to make it work for you, learn how to save well, spend well, invest it well.

 **Objectives**:

As a result of completing these activities you will be able to:

- **Gain a basic understanding of options for funding your business**
- **Establish expense tracking**
- **Identify places where you can save money to put this extra money towards your business**

Financials as a topic can make people incredibly nervous or stressed and I want to inspire you to think differently about the financials of your company. Yes, it takes a little bit of money to make money however you do not have to be a millionaire or independently wealthy to start your own business. Hopefully by now you know you just need an idea and the motivation to execute and the will to see it through. If you are concerned upfront with the amount of money it will take to start your business, there are several avenues to explore:

- Bootstrap – you raise/find/save your own money to pursue your business (this is the option I have elected to date)
- The 3 F's – Friends, Family & Fools
- Crowdfunding – online fundraising by telling your story and catalyzing major social media and email campaigns
- Bank Loans
- Grants – in general a large majority are only available for non-profit 501c3 organizations
- Angel Investors - private accredited investors
- Venture Capitalists – high tech focus, big money, want ownership and potentially a management role

Some of these methods I may explore in greater detail in separate courses however I want to re-emphasize the point – the numbers of your company tell a story. They are factual and data based – real information. In order to have a healthy business, you need to plan for things financially. Going through the steps of planning your business from a financial perspective can be incredibly insightful.

Activity 4.1

Business Expenses Table

The table below lists several basic business expenses. Look up each item and fill in the actual cost and frequency in which you will need to budget for covering this item. If you'd like to create your own business expenses table, a blank template can be found in the Resources section.

Item	Estimated Cost	Actual Cost with Frequency
Business email address	$5-15	$5.00 per month
Domain name	$10-20	$12.99 annual
Website – (lowest paid tier)	Free - $25 (a month?)	
Initial business bank account setup	$100-500	
P.O. Box	$___ per X months	
Filing with the State	$60	
Marketing collateral	$50	
Equipment/Supplies	$1000	
Software	$150	
Work phone	$50	

Activity 4.2

Extra Money Table

If you need to save a bit, what can you cut out to reach your financial goal sooner? Take a look at your daily, weekly and monthly spending habits. Is there anything you could eliminate or do without for a temporary period of time?

Below is a small sample list of activities to consider cutting current expenditure in order to save enough to invest in your own business. It can provide your financial reservoir. If you engage in any of the below activities, indicate the frequency next to the listed activity in the middle column by writing the letter of the frequency in the column as follows:

- D = Daily
- W = Weekly
- M = Monthly

A blank Extra Money Table template can be found in the Resources section.

Amount	Activity & Frequency	Total Monthly Amount in $
	Coffee, tea or other beverage	
	Eating out for lunch	
	Eating out for dinner	
	Beauty routines (manis, pedis, hair, etc.)	
	Playing games that cost money	
	Refurbishing your wardrobe	
	Monthly subscriptions	
	Other	
	Other	
	Other	
	Other	
GRAND TOTAL		

After that, write down how much you spend daily, weekly or monthly. Total the amount by the month. Remember if you indicated daily you will multiply the amount by 28 (assuming there are four seven day weeks to a month) and if you indicated weekly you are multiplying the amount by four. I want you to pin down your monthly expenditure on non-essential items so that you can see how easy it is to save the money you need to purchase your business supplies. You can make these changes if starting your own company is a priority.

One trait I have found in common with entrepreneurial women is that they are resourceful and creative. If you want to keep your costs down, I know you can do it. Also by leaning into other entrepreneurs, trusted friends, your Personal Advisory Team, they will be full of ideas and no doubt can help you find resources you didn't even know existed.

There are so many ways to cut costs, find good deals and make economically sound decisions. Remember you do not have to have your entire stock of supplies for an entire year before moving forward with the rest of your Launchpad Blueprint. This chapter in addition to encouraging you to do some research is equally to increase your *awareness*. You are building your business skills (budgeting, estimating cost of goods, expenses) and a strong foundation prior to your business launch. There is plenty more work to do and details to figure out.

Remember take one step each day to get closer to *your* definition of career freedom.

Intentionally left blank

MODULE 5
YOUR PLACE IN THE UNIVERSE

"Optimism is the faith that leads to achievement."

- Helen Keller

A business is a living thing that can truly take on a life of its own. There may be some bumps and hurdles along the way, however the toughest part sometimes is just getting started and if you worked through all the themes, concepts and activities presented in this guide, you are well on your way. What I have found over the years is that people often have wonderful, unique ideas that fill a gap in our society and world. Where these ideas stall is in the execution.

Execution is key. Knowing when to adapt and pivot, requires flexibility of mind. It may take time to learn these kinds of skills, however *entrepreneurship is a mindset* and the mind can be trained and expanded.

Objectives:

As a result of completing the activities you will be able to:
- **Complete the checklist of activities that needs to be completed for you to launch your business**
- **Prepare a "Pitch Deck" in order to fine tune your message about what you do**
- **Prepare a marketing promotions schedule**
- **Express gratitude in writing**

Activity 5.1

Systems Checklist

Below is a Systems Checklist to confirm you have everything you need to prepare for takeoff. Write in other items you have identified. A blank Systems Checklist template is located in the Resources section.

Check off when completed.	Items and/or Activities
	Name of business
	Domain name secured
	Business email account
	Registered business with the State
	Registered business with the IRS
	Business bank account
	Marketing strategy
	Business social media accounts

Supplies/equipment to build the product or systems for delivering the service	
Personal Advisory Group identified	
Local network or virtual network	
Expense recording sheet, app or online tool	
Money saved for the unexpected	
Insurance	

Activity 5.2

Your Pitch

You will want to be able to easily articulate what you do and most importantly why you built a business. People want to be inspired and moved and your passion can persuade others. There is an activity I want you to try in order to hone in on the essence of your business idea – prepare a presentation. You can use any presentation or slide show tool available such as Keynote, PowerPoint or Google Slides. The idea is to be concise enough that you could explain your business within five minutes. Use photos, graphics and words in place of sentences whenever possible.

Below are the slides I recommend you include:

1. Cover Slide
2. Problem/ Opportunity – passion point/ Inspiration
3. Your Idea – product/ services
4. Marketing – clients/ personas
5. Business Model - pricing

6. Growth
7. Competition
8. Team
9. Financials
10. Final Statement

This is a creative way to bring your whole idea together and prepare you for explaining your idea to anyone who asks about it. You will be more clear, confident and articulate if you dial in your messaging. Practice saying it out loud on your own time or in front of a mirror. Let the "pitch" become a natural part of discourse for you. When you tell people about your business idea, most likely they will be naturally curious and ask you questions about it. This is how word of mouth marketing can begin if someone really takes to your idea or wants to share it with others.

Activity 5.3

Schedule Initial Marketing Promotions

As you pull everything together that you've been working on during the course, you will want to create your initial launch messaging while identifying the best way(s) to promote your business. This ties back to your marketing plan and strategy. It is important to literally schedule marketing promotional activities on your calendar so you can prepare and plan accordingly. As mentioned in Module 3, specifically Activity 3.3, tools such as Hootsuite or Buffer can make this easy for you to manage. Many people, myself included, find marketing planning schedules easier to pursue when there are monthly or quarterly themes based around key events or your area of expertise. That way you don't have to keep thinking about different ways to approach your audience nor will you appear disjointed by sending a variety of messages across the channels.

For example, my company focuses on empowering women entrepreneurs. Themes I consider include:

- Skills building
- Lead with meaning
- Empowering oneself
- Working with a small budget

As you approach the final stages of getting ready to launch, the below are items you can prepare during final days, weeks or months. This all depends on the timeline in which you're planning to launch your business.

Pre-Launch Short Checklist (insert check next to item once completed.)

1. __ Finish content (website, social media content, images)
2. __ Obtain logo design and build website (keep private until launch date)
3. __ Finalize the product and/or service offering
4. __ Setup Social Media account #1 and reserve the business name on other accounts
5. __ Inform your network the launch is coming

When you literally map this out it will help you commit to getting things done every week. In general, when we put things in our calendars most people stick with it - you're literally making an appointment with yourself. Show up and don't be late!

Before you go live with your business launch, it is important to take some time to thank the people who helped you along the way. For some people, this may seem like an "old-fashioned" approach however no one goes this journey of entrepreneurship alone and it's important to acknowledge those who have supported you.

> **We need one another. People need to be appreciated and showing gratitude is a genuine gift you can give someone which costs you nothing except a little bit of thought and effort.**

Select one person from your Personal Advisory Team, your network or someone else altogether that you would like to thank for supporting you and your business initiative. Tell them what their support means to you.

5.4 Gratitude Letters

Letter to Supportive Person

Dear _____ ,

Sincerely,

The final activity is to write a short letter to yourself focusing on the positive attributes you have and applauding the effort you have made to work through this process. You can start it with Dear (insert your name), Dear Me or Hi (name), whatever suits your style. Congratulate yourself, compliment yourself, go all out and no holding back:

Letter to Self

Yours truly,

Remind yourself of your accomplishment. Feel good about the effort you have made and know you have empowered yourself.

CONCLUSION

"I'd rather regret the things I've done than regret the things I haven't done."

- Lucille Ball

You made it! YOU have worked through your ideation stage, customer profiling, created a marketing strategy, learned some basics about websites and business accounts and you have a product or service to sell to people. That took hard work and *determination*. Another way I like to look at it is that you have **grit**. This is a key characteristic of every entrepreneur I have ever encountered be it in Seattle, Hawaii, Kentucky or Colorado.

You may be surprised what happens with your business and hopefully it's the good kind of surprise! Know to expect some twists, turns and pivots. What is most important is that you do not give up! This will be one of the most rewarding, enriching, educational, and challenging adventures during your life's journey. As mentioned at the beginning of the last module, execution is key and knowing when to adapt and pivot, requires flexibility of mind. It may take time to learn these kinds of skills; however, it is possible. Remember *entrepreneurship is a mindset*.

You've checked off items on lists, filled in tables, conducted research, documented details and concluded with writing letters. It's time to launch your business or rather time to **launch to FREEDOM**. This is your time to shine. Shoot for the stars. All systems are a GO!

Launch your company!

"Done is better than perfect."
- Sheryl Sandberg

A Letter from the Founder to YOU

Dear Aspiring Woman Entrepreneur,

Now it is my turn to thank you. I appreciate you picking up this workbook, consuming its contents and hopefully learning something new. I have a list of ideas for future books and online courses, however I want to know that the resources I create are helpful to you. Please feel free to send me ideas of topics in which you desire more information for keeping your business running, scaling your business, or other topics and areas of interest from a woman in business. There are so many topics that can be further explored from leadership ideas to wellness, however if it's not meeting your needs or helping you solve problems, I am missing the mark of my mission which is to inspire women entrepreneurs to reach their aspirations. In support of this mission my goal is to provide resources that are easily accessible and affordable, so nothing stands in the way of your success.

I wish you the best of luck with your endeavor.

Sincerely,

Hope

ACKNOWLEDGEMENTS

I'd like to acknowledge the many people I've worked with over the years from the outstanding mentors, advisors and investors beginning with the LaunchPad initiative days in Seattle at the Center for Commercialization (yes, I remember all of you) to the numerous entrepreneurs I met in those days willing to take that first step outside of their comfort zone. Kudos to following that "silly idea," especially Preston Van Hooser, whose "misting station" was acquired after a few short years by a major medical device company. Spending those years working so closely with entrepreneurs including a couple of Gates Fellows cohorts from the Center for Entrepreneurship through the Foster School of Business at the University of Washington as well as watching extraordinary research based teams pitch, gave me the entrepreneurial itch.

When I look back over my early years, I remember my parents patience as I would create paper crafts and try to sell them to their invited dinner guests. The bookmarks were my favorite because doesn't everyone like to read and need a bookmark? From my very early days my parents have always supported my interests and allowed me to spread my wings many times over the years, to them I will always be grateful. Their love and support has been the bedrock of my foundation. My father for having entrepreneurial spirit and encouraging it in me. My mother for teaching me those "soft skills" that would truly make a difference later in life. My brothers for believing in me, sharing this vacillating journey called life and remembering to laugh. Life is short.

One of the best events to take root in the Fort Collins community is 1Million Cups, a Kauffman Foundation program. I have met so many people there who have touched my life in a variety of ways and if I had to sum it up, I would say they are some of the most creative, intelligent people I know. To name a few of those individuals who have touched me: Harrison Hand – creativity with a mission and further inspiration for this book, Nathalie Rachline – diligent inquisitiveness, steadfast and persistence, Andy Stoel – inspiration and taking risks literally around the world and Cindy Skalicky – communication, presentation and humor. I value the lessons they have each taught me and continue to do.

Another pinnacle moment in life is when I volunteered for the Biz Girls CEO Accelerator program founded by Peter Adams, Executive Director of the Rockies Venture Club (the longest operating angel investor group in our country.) This was a life - changing experience and being the Executive Director when the program became a stand-alone 501c3 non-profit entity, received two grants and attracted girls from four cities in Colorado to participate in the first week long program in Fort Collins will be forever etched in my mind. Those girls aged 15 to 18 rocked my world – creating their own businesses and pitching to a room full of adults – they did it! During this time, I was approached by numerous adult women who wanted to enroll in the Biz Girls program or would remark "I wish there was something like this when I was young." Based on all those comments from volunteers, guest speakers, mentors, coaches and workshop facilitators I realized there is an important yet underserved market in which I could offer information, knowledge and resources to empower women.

Shout out to the "Second Saturday" group as they are always supportive, inquisitive and have even helped vet some of my ideas, offered resources and encouragement to stay the course, even if the whole business concept was not completely baked after 100 days…

Extra props and kudos to my editorial team comprised of Don Hartman, Chas Hartman, Julie Gold, Mary Ann Hjelmfelt and Cindy Skalicky.

My family comprised of my husband, Denichiro "Denny" and son, Denshin you two are my world. Thank you for bringing so much joy into my life, creating new experiences each season and exploring new activities together. Words can't express what you mean to me, yet to have any opportunity to acknowledge all you have done, all you continue to do and how I respect and admire you both, is worth every bit of effort. I'm incredibly lucky and grateful. My heart is yours.

RESOURCES

"The most difficult thing is the decision to act, the rest is merely tenacity."

- Amelia Earhart

For additional resources please see my website Resources page. The page rotates resources based on the most current and relevant information available to help you on your journey:

http://www.escape-velocity.biz/

Inspirational Quotes

https://www.contentfac.com/25-quotes-that-will-inspire-entrepreneurial-women-to-kick-ass-in-business/

Entrepreneurial Meetup Group

1 Millions Cups
https://www.1millioncups.com/

How to Start a Business Websites

Small Business Administration https://www.sba.gov/

SCORE https://www.score.org/

Survey Tools
https://www.surveymonkey.com/

https://www.google.com/forms/about/

https://www.typeform.com/

Books
Lean In by Sheryl Sandberg

StrengthsFinder 2.0 by Tom Rath

Talk Like Ted by Carmine Gallo

Start With Why by Simon Sinek

Podcast
StartUp Podcast Season 1 - Gimlet

Social Media Management Tools

https://hootsuite.com/platform
https://buffer.com/

Articles
https://www.entrepreneur.com/article/38822

https://www.forbes.com/sites/garrettgunderson/2015/11/30/how-to-choose-the-right-legal-entity-for-your-business/#67b4c3f63512

https://www.businessnewsdaily.com/8163-choose-legal-business-structure.html

I encourage you to do some research on your own and to stay in the practice of doing so. It's empowering! In addition you can continue to build upon your business knowledge base by leveraging your Personal Advisory Team or a professional peer group. Knowledge is power!

Module 2 – Activity 2.1 Preparation Checklist Template

In the table below create a list of activities you need to complete before you are ready to launch your business. This can include long and short term activities. This is your initial "to-do" list.

Check When Completed	Activity

Activity 2.3 The Launchpad Blueprint Template

Work your way through each section below, filling in your initial responses. You may fine tune your responses over time.

What (Product/ Service)	Who (Customer Personas)	How (Market Channels)	Where (Store, Online)

Differentiator (Competitive Advantage)	Expenses (Costs of Supplies)	Competitors (Name 2-3)	Pricing (The cost)

Module 4 – Activity 4.1 Business Expenses Table

The table below lists several basic business expenses. Look up each item and fill in the actual cost and frequency in which you will need to budget for covering this item.

Item	Estimated Cost	Actual Cost with Frequency

Activity 4.2 Extra Money Table

Take a look at your daily, weekly and monthly spending habits. Indicate the frequency after the listed activity in the middle column by writing the letter of the frequency in the column as follows:

- D = Daily
- W = Weekly
- M = Monthly

Amount	Activity & Frequency	Total Monthly Amount in $
GRAND TOTAL		

Remember if you indicated daily you will multiply the amount by 28 (assuming there are four seven day weeks to a month) and if you indicated weekly you are multiplying the amount by four.

Module 5 - Activity 5.1 Systems Checklist Template

Below is a blank Systems Checklist to create and confirm you have everything you need to prepare for takeoff. Write in all items you have identified.

Check off when completed.	Items and/or Activities

You have considered and worked through several of the key pieces to get your business up and running. At this point there are a few nuts and bolts that need to be put into place. They are not necessarily creative in essence however they are necessary so that you can run a legitimate business. You will need to file your business name with your local state and then with the federal government. All you need to do is search for "Register new business in (name of state.)" Each state has a lot of information available on line to help walk you through the steps. Currently I live in Colorado and for example, the State of Colorado offers a checklist for new businesses and a Colorado business resource book. All of these resources are free and can empower you with tremendous insight as to what you may need to be aware of for your particular business industry.

Mostly I want you to be aware of taking these steps and note there are several kinds of business entities you can form. They all have tax implications and if you have an accountant, you may wish to seek her opinion or advice before filing. Otherwise be sure to read and understand the nuances of all of them so that you don't have to go through the hassle of changing your legal entity down the road.

If you come to this pass, it can be done, but will require additional forms, fees and you may have to wait a bit. This could be most critical if you start off bootstrapping and then realize you need to be for example an LLC instead of a sole proprietorship due to wanting to raise funds with accredited investors. If you know for a fact that you will need to raise funds, plan to raise funds, have other co-owners start off with the LLC.

In addition to tax implications there are several other factors you will want to consider when making your decision such as: liability, flexibility, complexity, control, capital investment, licenses/permits/regulations. Your legal structure will affect your annual tax reporting obligations and how you can operate so it's worth spending a little time weighing the options.

The below information is in no way legal or tax planning advice, and I highly recommend you consult with a certified accountant (CPA) and other tax or legal professionals. In case this is new territory for you, and to further build your business knowledge base, the five types of business entities are:

1. **Sole proprietorship** – single owner, 1 person, responsible for all profits and debts.

2. **Partnership** – owned by two or more individuals. 2 types: general – all shared equally and limited – one partner has control of the operations while the other person contributes and only receives part of the profit

3. **Limited Liability Company (LLC)**

A limited liability company is a hybrid structure that allows owners, partners or shareholders to limit their personal liabilities while enjoying the tax and flexibility benefits of a partnership

4. **Corporation**
   The law regards a corporation as an entity that is separate from its owners. It has its own legal rights, independent of its owners — it can sue, be sued, own and sell property, and sell the rights of ownership in the form of stocks.

5. **Cooperative**
   A cooperative is owned by the same people it serves. Its offerings benefit the company's members, who vote on the organization's mission and direction.

In regards to corporations, there are several types, including C corporations, S corporations, B corporations, close corporations, and nonprofit corporations. In case this is the type of business you need to form, see below for a summary of each type of corporation:

- **C corporations**, owned by shareholders, are taxed as separate entities.
- **S corporations,** much like partnerships or LLCs. Owners also have limited liability protection.
- **B corporations**, otherwise known as benefit corporations, are for-profit entities structured to make a positive impact on society.
- **Close corporations**, typically run by a few shareholders, are not publicly traded and benefit from limited liability protection.
- **Nonprofit corporations** exist to help others in some way, and are rewarded by tax-exemption.

Intentionally left blank

NOTES

"You can't give up! If you give up, you're like everybody else."

- Chris Evert